HAUNTED NORTHWEST GEORGIA

THE LEGEND OF THE GHOST HEARSE

AND OTHER SPOOKY TALES

Schiffer Publishing Ltd

4880 Lower Valley Road • Atglen, PA 19310

Other Schiffer Books on Related Subjects:

Georgia Spirits and Specters. Beth Dolgner. ISBN: 978-0-7643-3256-2.

Haunted History: Atlanta and North Georgia. Corinna Underwood. ISBN: 978-0-7643-2854-1.

Spirits of Georgia's Southern Crescent. Christina A. Barber. ISBN: 978-0-7643-2945-6.

Savannah Ghosts: Haunts of the Hostess City. David Harland Rousseau and Julie Collins Rousseau. ISBN: 978-0-7643-2494-9.

Library of Congress Control Number: 2016948652

Designed by Molly Shields

Type set in BarrettIronwork/Times New Roman

ISBN: 978-0-7643-5214-0
Printed in China

Published by Schiffer Publishing, Ltd.
4880 Lower Valley Road
Atglen, PA 19310
Phone: (610) 593-1777; Fax: (610) 593-2002
E-mail: Info@schifferbooks.com
Web: www.schifferbooks.com

For our complete selection of fine books on this and related subjects, please visit our website at www.schifferbooks.com. You may also write for a free catalog.

Schiffer Publishing's titles are available at special discounts for bulk purchases for sales promotions or premiums. Special editions, including personalized covers, corporate imprints, and excerpts, can be created in large quantities for special needs. For more information, contact the publisher.

We are always looking for people to write books on new and related subjects. If you have an idea for a book, please contact us at proposals@ schifferbooks.com.

To my daughter, Haley—living proof of
God's love and unmerited grace.
I love you beyond words.

CONTENTS

Acknowledgments...................................5
Author Note...7
Preface..8

Chapter 1: Floyd County........................11
   The Narrows....................................11
   Ruby..14
   Opera Alley......................................17
   The Baby in the Cemetery..............19
   Spirits of Reeceburg Road...............20
   The Old Coosa House......................25
   The Chieftains Museum...................28

Chapter 2: Bartow County.....................33
   Allatoona Pass.................................33

Chapter 3: Chattooga County................37
   A Nice House in the Country...........37
   The Horse-Drawn Hearse...............39
   Company's Coming..........................40
   Ola Mae..42
   The Man in the Tan Coat................44
   The Berryton House.........................45
   The Child in the Fog........................47

Chapter 4: Whitfield County...................51
   The Blue Hole..................................51

Chapter 5: Gordon County.....................55
   Resaca Confederate Cemetery......55

Chapter 6: Catoosa County....................59
   The Soldiers....................................59

Chapter 7: Dade County.........................63
   Guardian Ghost of the Canyon.....63

Chapter 8: Just over the Line:
Northeast Alabama................................67
   Ghosts of Chesterfield....................67
   Granny Dollar and Buster...............69
   Little River Canyon.........................72

Chapter 9: Undisclosed Location...........77
   The Nursing Home...........................77

Bibliography and Recommended
Reading..79

ACKNOWLEDGMENTS

There are so many people to thank in the creation of this book, I don't know where to start. Thanks to Mike Ragland, author and historian, for taking me under your wing and helping me get started. I don't know where I'd have been without your help and guidance. Thank you for answering my endless questions and for pointing me in the right direction.

Thanks to Tommy Tatum for being a proofreader and cheerleader (and neighbor, fellow book lover and friend). I am so blessed to have you near by!

I would not have many of the stories in the book without the wonderful Debby Brown. There was never a kinder, more fascinating woman in the history of Floyd County. She was indeed a treasure. The Lord called her home before this book was finished. (It seems the angels love to hear a good story, also.) She is greatly missed and will never be forgotten. I think of her often.

Thanks to Matt Wnorowski, Adam Dean, and Kelly Miller of Southern States Paranormal. I am so lucky to work with these sweet guys. Thanks for answering my questions, telling me your stories, and including me in your group.

To Jamie Cavin, civil war enthusiast and expert on all things Menlo. Thanks for answering my questions (even the same ones over and over.) To Barbara Hammett, and everyone on the Menlo, Georgia, Facebook Page. No wonder Menlo is such a great town—its citizens are some of the nicest people I've met.

To Khevin Farmer and Billy Gilliland, fellow classmates and cheerleaders for my cause. Thanks for encouraging me onward when I felt stuck. Love you both, my friends.

Of course, I have to thank all the followers on my Facebook pages, Ghosts of Northwest Georgia and Shadows in the Pines. Thanks also to those who follow my web page www.bethyoungblood.com. I love your stories, your comments, your insights, your ideas, and most of all, your enthusiasm. You've got me through many episodes of writer's block and discouragement. You guys are awesome!

To Joy Cleghorn, my former co-worker and a gifted writer. Thanks for your stories.

Also, to Ted Carver, and to Dianne Rittenhouse for introducing us. Thanks for your stories and advice.

To my parents for encouraging me to write what I love, and to read, read, read. Thanks for those Sunday afternoons of babysitting so I could write. (I'm sure you didn't mind that at all—wink.)

Thanks to my friends who have supported me in every phase of this journey. Thanks for your help, your advice, your encouragement, and for lending an ear and urging me on.

Lastly, thanks to those of you who shall remain anonymous for sharing your intimate and treasured stories with me. I know many of you risked losing a job, ridicule from friends and neighbors, and just plain wondering what people would think. Each of you is a treasure to me. Many of you I am now proud to refer to as my friend. That, in itself was a blessing.

"There are more things in heaven and earth,
Horatio, than are dreamt of in your philosophy."
—William Shakespeare

AUTHOR NOTE

Many of the stories in this book occurred on private property. Many occurred in cemeteries, which although not private, are sacred grounds. Please use respect when visiting any haunted area. Make sure you have permission from the property owner before you visit private property. Treat all areas with respect and leave them better than you found them. Vandalism and disrespect are never acceptable in any place.

The stories in this book, although believed to be true by the teller, cannot be verified. They are a part of the local lore of the area.

PREFACE

Ghost stories and the south seem to go together. The south carries an air of mystery. Centuries-old home places, abandoned graveyards—legends and ghosts abound here. The south moves at it's own speed, a little slower than the rest of the world. Ghosts are as natural here as pine trees and sweet tea.

I grew up on a family farm in the mountains of Northwest Georgia. Here in the foothills of Appalachia, time moves at a different pace. Tradition and custom run strong. Storytelling is an art here, and my daddy was a storyteller indeed. True storytellers are born, not created in a class in some night school. They are trained at the feet of their elders on front porches, by firesides, around campfires. Storytelling has been a pure form of entertainment here for centuries and, if you look hard enough, the masters do still exist.

When I was growing up, I loved listening to my daddy's stories. A true storyteller, you can't just walk up and say, "Tell me the story of…" The setting must be created. The time and mood must be right. This is how it is with all true storytellers. There comes that moment when all the dishes are put away and everyone sits on the porch or retires around the fire for the evening. A quiet settles in. A comfortable silences settles over everyone. Finally, those magical words appear…"You know, one time…" or "Did I ever tell you about the time when…" That's when the stories come.

As a child, this was my favorite time as the shadows begin to grow and the cicadas begin their summer song. The little ones start to fall asleep. The grown-ups were relaxed and, if I was quiet, they'd think I was asleep or, at least, not paying attention. The best stories always came late. At first, there were funny stories, thoughtful stories, sad stories and, always, hunting stories. The hunting stories gave way to that-thing-that-happened-that-could-not-be-explained-on-a-hunting-trip and, finally, this lead to the spookier ones. Then came the tales of the unexplained. The tales that left you thinking—and a little bit frightened. The tales that made you check under your bed one extra time. These tales were always my favorite.

My daddy knew instinctively how to tell a tale—when to pause to give you time to think, to picture the story, to draw your own conclusions. He knew how to build up to the scariest part, and was likely as not to leave you laughing as he was to leave you scared to turn off your bedside lamp. My daddy could tell a story.

I don't profess to have my daddy's talent. If I only had a tiny portion, I would consider myself blessed. However, I love a good ghost tale. I've loved them since I was a child devouring every scary book the Chattooga County Library had to offer. It's a love that never left me. It comes to me honestly, this love of a good ghost tale.

In these pages I've collected stories from people who have had their own encounters with the unexplained. Are they true? Well, all I can say is this: each of these tales was told to me in earnest. The teller sincerely believed the tale to be true. You won't find many of the well-known places and traditional stories you may find in other books about Northwest Georgia. I sought to find the lesser-known tales. I tried to talk to eyewitnesses when possible. Whether you are a lover of the supernatural, or just a lover of a good tale well told, I hope you enjoy these stories. Please remember: a small part of a real person's heart and soul went into the telling of each one.

CHAPTER ONE

FLOYD COUNTY

The Narrows
Coosa Community
ROME, GA

A four-lane stretch of Highway 20 rolls lazily out of western Floyd County, Georgia, between Turnip and Heath Mountains into Western Alabama. Travelers on this lonely road may not be aware that, just a few years ago, this was a two-lane winding road—one of the deadliest in Northwest Georgia. According to an April 26, 1991, article in the "Comment and Opinion" section of the *Rome News Tribune*, in a two-year period alone there were nineteen wrecks and four fatalities on this lonely stretch of road. Later, in another *Rome News Tribune* article, on February 15, 1998, "Police Know Stretch of Ga. 20 As Danger Zone," J. W. Humphries reported twenty-seven more wrecks between 1996 and 1998 and four more fatalities. Local law enforcement blamed the wrecks on the road itself. Drivers came into the area at a high rate of speed, unaware of the treacherous curves ahead. Maybe they were right, but there are others in the area who blame the tragedies on a far more sinister reason.

Old timers will tell you that this lonely stretch of valley was feared when only wagons and the occasional stagecoach traveled the path that later became known as The Narrows. In those day, the valley was much different than it is today. A dirt wagon path ambled down the lonely valley between Turnip and Heath through dark woodlands with hills rising up

A newly widened GA 20 begins its passage through "The Narrows." c. 2015. *Courtesy David Jefferson Davis Jr.*

sharply on each side. Bandits took great advantage of this isolated area, robbing many a stagecoach and lone traveler.

In those days, a huge boulder sat up on the side of the road. So large was the boulder that the road curved itself outward around it. That is where *she* sat. No one knew where she had come from, or what caused her to appear there on certain evenings, her long dark hair flowing over her shoulders, her dark dress spread out around her. They say she could cast a spell with her eyes. Those unlucky enough to fall under her gaze would become paralyzed and helpless. The horses would go mad from fear, running recklessly out of the valley, the driver unable to move or speak until the horses, foaming and breathless, finally brought them out of The Narrows. The driver wouldn't be able to remember a thing after seeing her. Numerous riders told of their hands being frozen, unable to hold the reins as the frightened horse fled in fear from the phantom on the rock.

Debby Brown's great-grandmother had a firsthand experience with the woman on the rock when she was a young girl growing up in the valley. The child of a wealthy planter, she traveled The Narrows with her family for a trip to town one sunny day. For families out in the country, a trip into town was a rare event. The long trip required rising before daylight and starting out just as the sun began to peek over the horizon. Farm life was lonely, and town trips were a social event. Families packed a lunch and spent the day browsing shops, catching up on the latest news, and visiting with friends. This day was no exception. The sun was beginning to dip into the evening sky as the family left town and headed back toward the valley.

The night was pitch black as the horse-drawn buggy entered The Narrows. The only sound to be heard in the darkness was the sound of the horses' feet on the dirt path. As the buggy rounded a bend in the road, the family saw a strange glow coming from the boulder up ahead. As the buggy came even with the boulder, they saw her. Her long black dress flowed out over the rock as she turned to stare at the buggy. The young girl stared up in fear as the woman looked down at the helpless family. For the rest of her life she would tell of the woman's piercing eyes as they stared directly into her own. She and everyone else in the buggy were paralyzed. They couldn't move or speak as the buggy rattled at break-neck speed along the isolated road out of The Narrows and into the valley beyond.

Not until they were safely out of the area were they again able to move and speak. They sat in stunned silence, their minds almost unable to comprehend what had just happened. None of them ever forgot that night, or the penetrating eyes of the phantom woman on the rock.

The two-lane highway known as The Narrows was finally widened into the four-lane road it is today. Cars drive back and forth between Georgia and Alabama past green pastures and farmland. The boulder that sat by the road is no longer there. But, quite possibly, the phantom woman may still be there on dark nights . . . waiting. If you find yourself driving through The Narrows on a lonely, dark night and you see a faint glow up ahead, be careful not to look.

A bend in GA 20 near where the phantom was seen, c. 2015. *Courtesy David Jefferson Davis Jr.*

Ruby
DeSoto Theater
ROME, GA

The Historic DeSoto Theatre, 530 Broad Street, is one of Rome's most well-known historical buildings. The first venue of the south designed and built for sound pictures, this "talkie" theatre opened its doors in August 1929. O. C. Lam, the theatre's owner, named the theatre for Hernando DeSoto, who was thought to have passed through Rome in 1540. Seating over 1,000 patrons, the DeSoto was one of the seven largest movie theatres in Georgia when it opened. The theatre boasted modern heating and cooling systems, as well as a state-of-the art fire safety system. For the next fifty years, the theatre served as a primary source of entertainment for the surrounding area.

DeSoto closed its doors as a movie theater in 1982, but was soon reopened by the Rome Little Theatre Company. Serving as a venue for plays and film festivals, the theatre remains one of Rome's top entertainment spots. However, the actors and actresses performing at the theatre have come to realize that not all the patrons at the Desoto are of the human kind.

The historic DeSoto Theatre, c. 2015.
Courtesy of David Jefferson Davis Jr.

The Great Depression hit the Rome area hard, as it did in the rest of the nation. Jobs and money were scarce as families struggled to survive. Young and old were affected by the hard times, and many sought an escape, however brief, from the sadness and struggle surrounding them daily. One of those was Ruby.

Ruby was around seven years old when the Depression settled on her community in South Rome like a black cloud. A nice neighborhood in that time, South Rome provided a safe area for Ruby's large family to reside, but money was scarce. The oldest of several brothers and sisters, Ruby assisted her mother in the daily care of the younger siblings. As a reward, once a week, Ruby's mother would give her money for fare to take the streetcar down to the DeSoto Theatre for a day at the movies.

Ruby would arrive before the movies started in order to take her favorite seat down front. From this vantage point, Ruby escaped into a world of make believe. The cartoons, the newsreels, the picture shows . . . Ruby loved them and memorized them all. That evening, when the theatre closed its doors for the day, Ruby would take the streetcar back home to her family. As the family gathered together after dinner that night, Ruby would be the center of attention as the regaled her siblings with every detail of her day's adventure. A natural storyteller, Ruby made her siblings feel as if they, too, had been to a day at the movies.

One morning, as Ruby stepped off the streetcar and headed to the DeSoto for the day, she was hit by a passing automobile. A crowd gathered around the stunned little girl. To the crowd's relief, Ruby soon stood up and declared herself to be unharmed. In those days, there was no 911, and few families could afford a doctor. Internal injuries were largely unknown to the common person. As Ruby appeared to be okay, the crowd parted and allowed her to continue on to the DeSoto for a day at the movies. After settling into her favorite seat, Ruby began her day's adventures on the big screen.

Later that day, as the curtains closed and the crown began to depart, a young woman approached an usher. She was very concerned about a little girl who had been sitting beside her. The girl did not get up as the rest of the crowd began to leave the theater. Instead, she stared transfixed at the now-silent screen. When the woman tried to speak with her, the girl remained unresponsive. Fearing that the child was sick, she hurried the usher to the little girl's side. He immediately recognized Ruby as a regular patron and tried to wake her by gently shaking her. Instead of waking up, Ruby fell to the floor, dead. As she fell, her trolley token fell out of her hand and hit the floor. To this day, it has never been found.

These days, patrons to the DeSoto hear mysterious voices when no one else is present. Footsteps follow actors and workers as they walk up the stairs. Doors open and shut on their own. A small, dark shadow is seen darting in and out of the recesses of the theatre.

Several people working on the set for productions have found themselves to be the victim of a prankster. They leave the theatre from the back, leaving the door unlocked. Returning, they find the door to be locked from the inside.

Debby Brown recalled several strange experiences in the theatre while working on the set for various productions. Often, while washing out her paint brushes in a sink backstage, she would see a small, dark figure dart by at the end of the backstage hallway. When her children were small, she would often take them with her to work on the sets. She never liked to be alone in the theatre, especially after midnight.

One night, Debby's children were trying on costumes with the children of some other people working on the set. When it was time to leave, her son Quinten could not find the blue shirt he had worn to the theatre. Debby told him it was probably mixed in with the costumes, so he continued to search. After an hour had passed, the shirt had still not surfaced. An upset Quinten called Debby in to help him search, pointing to the place where his blue shirt was last seen. When a continued search turned up nothing, an exhausted Debby gave up. She told Quinten to wear another shirt home and they would wash it and return it tomorrow. For Quinten, this simply would not do. This was his favorite shirt. Standing in the costume room he called out, "Look! I want my blue shirt and I want it now!" and he stalked out of the room. He left the room and went to the top of the stairs, calling to his mother, "I gave her an ultimatum! I better get my shirt!" When he returned to the room a short while later, the shirt was folded neatly, lying on the chair where Quinten had placed it earlier. No one else had been in the room.

Quinten had an even closer brush with Ruby a few years later. After a show, Debby, Quinten, her daughter Mollie, and another actor stood behind the seats in back of the theatre, looking at the stage. They were getting ready for the upcoming play, which Quinten would direct and Debby would produce. All the lights in the theatre had been turned off for the night. The only light on the stage was shining from the streetlights on Broad Street. Glancing at Quinten, Debby noticed a strange look on his face. She describes it as "absolutely the weirdest look on his face I've ever seen." Never taking his eyes from the stage, he simply stated, "Let's get out of here." Looking in the direction of his gaze, they tried to see what he was seeing, but saw nothing. When asked what he saw, he only replied," Let's just get out of here." They got out of the theatre as quickly as they could. Once they were settled in their car, Quinten said, "I want to tell you what I saw. I saw her!" He had been looking at the stage when, suddenly, the white face of a little girl appeared. She had looked right at him. She had looked at him for several minutes before it dawned on him what he was actually seeing. Later on, he said to his mother, "I just thought of something. What if she wanted me to help her or something?" His mother asked if he wanted to go back inside. He replied, "No!"

Was the little girl that Quinten saw actually Ruby? Why does she remain at the DeSoto? Is she searching for her lost streetcar token so that she can return home? Or is she simply choosing to remain where she had her happiest moments?

Opera Alley
Broad Street
ROME, GA

In 1880, Mitchell Albert Nevin opened the Nevin Opera House on Rome's Broad Street. Standing four stories tall, the Nevin Opera House was a grand palace in its time, with seating for 1,000 and standing room for 200 more. The interior was lavish with the latest gas lamps, private boxes, elegant frescoes, and beautifully carved woodwork.

The Nevin was host to some of the finest musicians and actors in the country. Many local performers and vaudeville troupes performed there as well. There were concerts, plays, political events, and novelty shows. In order to accommodate his performers, Nevin had a side entrance and stairway added off an alley that ran beside the opera house. This allowed performers to enter and exit the opera house without using the main entrance. This alley became known as Opera Alley.

For more than thirty-five years the Nevin Opera House was one of the premier showplaces in the south. However, the Opera House's popularity began to decline as silent movie theatres began to open in Rome. After Nevin died in 1895, the Opera House changed hands several times before finally being condemned by the city in 1915. In the early morning hours of 1919, a fire broke out in the building. Firemen were able to save neighboring buildings, but the Nevin was gone forever.

Opera Alley is all that remains of the Nevin's heyday. Serving as a shortcut to Broad Street from a nearby parking deck, the alley has a great deal of foot traffic daily. It has also served as a backdrop for many photo shoots. Most people who pass beneath the iron archway are not aware of the alley's history or its significance to the city. Some, however, receive a chilly reminder that Opera Alley has a past, and, for some, the show still goes on.

Lavinia Willoby arrived in Rome with a troupe of actors and actresses slated to perform a variety of shows for several nights. After each night's performance, wealthy families would allow the troupe members to stay in their carriage and guest houses for the night. Lavinia was staying with one such family in a nearby home. Each night, the family driver would escort Lavinia to the Nevin in the family's carriage and, after the show, deliver her again to their guest house.

One fateful evening, Lavinia got into the carriage and headed out to her nightly performance. As the carriage rounded a corner, something went horribly wrong. Though the actual cause of the incident has been lost in time, no one disputes that there was indeed a horrible accident. Lavinia was thrown from the buggy and was killed instantly. She never made it to her performance . . . or did she? Local legend says that Lavinia is still trying to make it to her performance at the Nevin.

Mike Ragland was a police officer walking his beat in 1968. Part of his duty was to check the front doors of each business as he walked down Broad Street, then check the back doors as he walked back up First Street. He often took a shortcut, walking through Opera Alley. One evening, as he was coming up Opera Alley, he suddenly noticed that the air was colder around him. He was overcome with an eerie feeling. That's when he heard it: a *tap-tap-tap*—quiet at first, then louder as it approached him. He said it sounded like someone running in high heels. The *tap-tap-tap* came closer and closer until it was right upon him, but he couldn't see a thing. Suddenly, it sped past with a cold rush of icy wind that swept over the bewildered police officer.

Opera Alley on Rome's Broad Street once served as a backstage entrance to the Nevin Opera House. Modern visitors often get a chilly reminder of the alley's past as Lavinia Willoby rushes to her last performance, c. 2015. *Courtesy of David Jefferson Davis Jr.*

Afterward, he told his partner on the beat what had happened. The other officer laughed. It seems Mike was not the first to encounter the ghost of Opera Alley.

In more recent times, a young woman was jogging in the area and decided to cut through Opera Alley. She, too, heard the tapping of tiny heels and felt the icy wind rush past her. "I don't know what it was," she said, "but I never cut through that alley again!"

The next time you are walking along Broad Street, browsing the quaint shops and restaurants, take a short walk down Opera Alley. You just might meet Lavinia Willoby as she tries to make it to her next performance.

The Baby in the Cemetery
Coosa Community

It was a balmy evening in August 1920 when the congregation concluded their service and stepped out into the church yard. A quiet uneasiness hung in the air. Children who normally ran about the yard playing games and laughing loudly hung close to their mothers. Women stood with babies on hips whispering among themselves. The menfolk formed their own circles, talking quietly of crops and livestock. Now and then, someone would glance furtively into the cemetery, then glance away again quickly.

Tonight was the night it always happened. No one knew when it had started, or even why. All their lives, from generation to generation the story was passed down. It always came on an August night. Tonight was the night. Some of the adults laughed among themselves, joking about what they might see, most not really believing.

Mae Higgins was five years old that summer evening. As she stood listening to the adults tell the story of the phantom child that walked the church yard on a certain August night, she looked warily into the cemetery. Was it true?

Suddenly someone yelled, "Look! There it is!" A hush fell about the crowd as everyone turned to stare into the cemetery. Her uncle picked her up and put her on his shoulders so she could get a better view. What she witnessed in the quiet church yard that August evening would follow her all the days of her life. It played over and over again in her memory, never changing, even as she shared the story with her own grandchildren years later.

The story, it turns out, was true. There among the gravestones stood a small toddler. Pale, and wearing a long white gown, the child took no notice of the stunned congregation as it made its way through the cemetery and approached the horses, buggies, and wagons waiting nearby. The horses became panicked as the phantom child walked right beneath their feet. They began stomping and rearing up in their efforts to get away from the child. Still not noticing, the pale apparition made its way beneath the horses and wagons and into the woods beyond.

The congregation watched in stunned silence as the phantom entered the woods surrounding the church yard and quietly disappeared. Many had claimed not to believe in ghosts. So what had they all just seen?

Who is the phantom child that walks among the tombstones one evening every August? Where did it come from? Where is it going? Is it trying to return to its home? Is it looking for loved ones left behind? No one will ever know. But those who have stood and watched the silent specter make its way through the church yard on a summer evening will never forget.

Spirits of Reeceburg Road
Lindale, GA

It was a rainy summer evening in the 1940s. A young preacher slowly drove his red Chevrolet toward the tiny Floyd County community of Lindale. He and his six fellow passengers, all women, were headed to work on the night shift at the local textile mill. The rain gradually ended and a heavy fog descended upon the area as the group made their way down Reeceburg Road.

They were approaching a railroad crossing at New Bethel Cemetery. The fog was so thick the young reverend had to turn off his headlights in order to see if a train was coming down the tracks. Normally, this would have left the car in complete darkness. Instead, the car was engulfed in a bright light—a huge bonfire had suddenly appeared and was burning in the middle of the road just ahead of the car! Around twenty-five railroad crossties had been piled in the road and were burning in a fire so large that flames leapt into the night sky.

Screams came from the back seat. Where had the fire come from? It wasn't there two seconds ago. Dumfounded, the young man pulled the light switch again. As the car lights came on, the fire disappeared. The group sat in stunned silence. What had just happened here? They couldn't all have imagined the same thing. They had all seen a raging fire right in front of them. Now there was nothing but darkness . . . and an eerie silence.

He turned off the lights again. Again, the raging fire appeared, sending sparks high into the night. He quickly turned on the lights. It was gone. One of the ladies in the back began to cry. What was going on here? This could not be happening.

He turned off the lights again. Again, a roaring fire appeared in front of the car. Well, that did it. He was ready to get out of there. He turned on the lights again to make ready to leave. This time, however, the fire remained, towering into the sky and burning bright as ever.

The young man had seen enough. Against the protests of his passengers, he got out of the car and slowly approached the fire. He walked closer, until he could feel the heat from it on his face. Strange, it really didn't seem all that hot, compared to the size of the fire. He definitely felt the heat, but a fire that size should have been much hotter.

He inched his way around the fire and onto the dirt road leading into the cemetery. He stood on the gravel road on the lonely, foggy night staring at the strange fire and wondering what it all meant. As he stood pondering the fire, he gradually became aware of an odd sound in the distance. He listened closer. It was coming from the other side of the fire and was moving rapidly toward him. He couldn't believe his ears. Could it be? It was! The sound moving toward him was a galloping horse. He could hear what sounded like trace chains clanging behind the beast as it came nearer. Used by loggers to snake timber out of the forest, the sound was a familiar one to the preacher.

The horse was now running straight toward him through the fog at an alarming speed. He braced himself, not sure which way to turn in order to avoid being run over. He could hear it's panting breath. The chains were clanging loudly as they drug along the dirt road. Suddenly, he realized, as the beast thundered toward him, there was no horse! He could hear it, but it just….wasn't there. He felt a rush of air as the invisible horse crashed past him and on into the foggy night.

The chains rang out into the distance as the frightened man quickly made his way back to the car. He turned on the lights and sped away from the scene as quickly as possible. The ladies in the car peppered him with questions, but he had no answers. He could not explain what he had seen in that cemetery, but he would never, ever forget.

The next morning, on their way home from the mill. The group stopped again at the cemetery. They saw no hoofprints, no charred wood, nothing remaining from the scene they had witnessed the night before. It was as if it had never happened at all.

New Bethel Cemetery on Reeceburg Road in Lindale, c. 2015.

Although tracks no longer cross this section of Reeceburg Road, trains can still be heard here rolling through the night, c. 2015. *Courtesy David Jefferson Davis Jr.*

None of the friends ever found an explanation for the events, although, fifty years later, they still remembered the night clearly. They weren't the only ones to see the mysterious fire on Reeceburg Road. Many engineers on the Central of Georgia witnessed the bonfire as they passed through the area. After slamming on the brakes, a few even got out to investigate. The fire always disappeared as they got near.

Some witnesses have even heard a ghost train that passes through the area. The train whistle blows and the engine can be heard as it rolls down the tracks to parts unknown. However, no train can be seen.

Mysterious lights are seen darting about the railroad tracks. The lights are many-colored and dance through the air in a haphazard fashion. No explanation for the phenomena has ever been found.

Many others have reported hearing a horse pulling a wagon through the cemetery. Those brave enough to stay have heard the horse's breath and heard the creaking wheels of a wagon as it rolled right by them.

Evidently the apparitions in the cemetery aren't the only ones to haunt the tiny town of Lindale. On July 16, 1914, the *Weekly Times Recorder* in Americus, Georgia, reported that on July 13, a ghost had been appearing at midnight each night near the powerhouse of the Georgia Railway and Power Company. One of the witnesses was the Reverend J. E. Smith, pastor of Lindale Baptist Church. Reverend Smith described the apparition as being, "about the size and shape of a white calf or large dog." As Rev.

Smith passed through the area, the apparition appeared directly in front of him. It disappeared as quickly as it had appeared, leaving no trace.

A posse of armed volunteers set out to find the apparition, as it was causing much upset in the neighboring mill village. No trace was ever found.

If you visit the tiny village of Lindale during the day, you will find it to be a peaceful, friendly community. But if you go after dark you may get more than you bargained for. Please remember to respect private property as well as public, and leave the area just as you found it.

Mysterious lights, phantom trains, and an unidentified apparition have haunted these tracks near the community of Lindale since the 1800s, c. 2015. *Courtesy of David Jefferson Davis Jr.*

The Old Coosa House
Coosa, GA

The house stood on a rise just off the Alabama Road (Georgia Highway 20) as it runs through the Coosa community near where the entrance to Inland Container is today. Standing two stories tall with a chimney at both ends and columns proudly lining its porches, the house was a testament to the wealth and prosperity of the family that built it in the early 1800s. By the time it was torn down in the 1970s, the house had become so well known that people from as far away as Texas came to visit. It wasn't the beauty of the house that drew the visitors, however. It was a ghost.

The story began at the turn of the century when a young teen named Lisbeth lived there with her family. Beautiful and cultured, Lisbeth had all the privileges her family's wealth provided. When Lisbeth fell in love with John, the poor son of a local farmer, her family was appalled. They opposed the relationship and forbade the two from seeing one another. Still, as the young and in love will do, the pair continued to meet secretly in the nearby woods.

Rumors began to surface. Her family heard that John had even given Lisbeth a ring. They confronted her and told her she was forbidden to wear any ring from the likes of that poor farmhand. They would have taken the ring from her, but it had mysteriously disappeared. Try as they might, they couldn't find it anywhere.

At that time, the Coosa area was remote. There were no nearby hospitals. Doctors made house calls, if the family could afford a doctor. Many families depended on home remedies. When Lisbeth became ill, her father summoned a doctor immediately. The doctor informed the family that Lisbeth had contracted typhoid fever. Distraught, they tended the bedridden Lisbeth round the clock. In her delirium, she begged repeatedly to see John. She banged on her bedroom wall, night and day, begging and crying for her beloved John. Her family would not allow John to come into their house, however. Instead, he would stand silently in the nearby woods where they had once met. From this secret spot, he could see her bedroom window. Here he stood a silent vigil for the girl he loved, right up until the day she died.

It was after Lisbeth's death that strange things began to happen in the home. At first, a loud thumping noise would awaken the family late at night. Later, Lisbeth's voice could still be heard wailing and calling from her room. A loud banging noise would start in the room and then travel down the hallway. Eventually the noises could even be heard during the day.

Friends and neighbors came to witness the phenomena. As word spread, more and more people came to visit. The family even started charging admission. An article in a national magazine spurred travelers from as far away as Texas. Wagons, buggies, and later, motor cars would line the highway.

Lisbeth remained invisible, although her voice could be heard plainly. When asked to show herself, she would reply, "No, that wouldn't do." One day, the voice commanded family members to look behind the mantle of the fireplace in her room. They did as she commanded. In a tiny hiding place tucked into the wall, they found a watch and bracelet along with the ring John had given her. The ring fell to the floor and rolled away. Although family members searched for years, the ring was never seen again.

The haunting continued throughout the years. As Lisbeth's family members died or moved away, the house sat empty. Periodically, the house would be lived in by other family members and was eventually rented out. However, no one could stay in the house for very long. Neighbors recalled seeing lights in the house at night, even though no one was living there at the time. A family member later recalled that, as he worked in the fields near the house, he often saw a light in the windows of the house, although there was no electricity running to the house at all.

In a news article from 1991, an elderly woman recalled living in the house with her family in 1920. She was seven years old at the time. According to her interview, she was working on her lessons with her siblings one night in the upstairs room that had once been Lisbeth's. When a heavy knocking began downstairs, they thought someone was breaking into their house. When her father called out to the intruders, the knocking came up the stairs, into the room, and went around the bed.

She remembered people coming from all over the country to witness the haunting. Even after she and her family moved out of the house the next year, her grandparents and uncle remained behind, living in the house until the 1950s. They called in paranormal investigators, but no cause was ever found. They continued to be plagued with the wailing, knocking, and jingling of bedsprings until they, too, left the home in the 1950s.

In another news article from 1973, a former renter recalled that lights would suddenly turn on and off while he shaved each morning. He, too, experienced unidentified noises in the home. The same article reported two people who had been sleeping upstairs in the home came rushing down the stairs during the night and left the house. Later, they claimed to have felt ghostly hands touching their faces and running through their hair. Still others complained of having the covers pulled off while they slept.

The home was torn down in the 1970s to make room for the widening of the Alabama Road. No one had lived inside the house for many years. A local young man was working with the DOT on the project. He and a co-worker decided to go in the famous house and see it for themselves before it was gone forever. He had grown up hearing tales of the house from his grandmother. His great-uncle had been one of the witnesses to the haunting in the early years after Lisbeth's death.

As the house sat in silence awaiting its fate, the two men entered the main room and looked around. Standing in the large room surrounded by an eerie silence, they stared up at the enormous staircase that led to the second floor. Vandals had left their mark. A mantelpiece had been torn from the wall and lay upon the floor. Debris lay scattered about the inside of the once-beautiful home.

Quietly they approached the staircase. As soon as they began to climb the stairway, an overwhelming sense of foreboding surrounded the men. The closer they came to the top of the stairs, the stronger the feeling became. It seemed they were surrounded by a thick cloud of despair. It almost made walking difficult, as if something intentionally held them back. Was Lisbeth aware that her home was about to be torn down? Did she know that her hundred-year vigil for John had come to naught—that he was lost forever more? Maybe she just needed these last minutes alone in her home to remember and to grieve. A hundred years of a heartache so strong it crossed the barriers of time and space filled the house. For whatever reason, the men felt as if they were walking in a thick cloud of sadness. Finally, just down the hall from Lisbeth's room, they stopped. They looked at each other and wordlessly turned around. They knew they could go no further. It was as if a physical force was preventing them from walking any further. Silently, they retreated down the stairs, leaving Lisbeth to spend her last day at home in peace. No humans ever entered the house again. It was torn down to make room for Highway 20.

An entire generation has grown up in the Coosa community not knowing the familiar sight of the grand old home. Yet, the older ones remember.

The Chieftains Museum
Rome, GA

Sitting in the quiet shade of centuries-old oak trees, this magnificent home seems out of place amidst the government buildings and daily traffic on Rome's busy Riverside Parkway. Yet, when Major Ridge and his family moved here around 1794, this was a 200-acre farm. He built a two-story dog trot cabin that was modernized through the years into the grand home we see today. He also added a ferry and trading post. Once a Cherokee warrior, Ridge became a leading statesman. While living here, Ridge participated in establishing the Cherokee government and served as speaker of the Cherokee National Council.

Chieftains Museum, Rome, Georgia, c. 2015. *Courtesy of Davis Jefferson Davis Jr.*

As Georgia began surveying Cherokee land for distribution in the Cherokee Land Lottery, Ridge was witness to more and more abuse upon his people by encroaching white settlers. Although Ridge had staunchly opposed removal in the past, he began to rethink his views on removal and made the monumental decision to negotiate a treaty with the US government. He felt that removing his people from the impending turmoil was the only way to save the Cherokee Nation. This treaty resulted in what is now known as the Trail of Tears. Because of his signing the treaty, Ridge, his son, and his nephew were killed by other Cherokees in 1839.

In 1971, the Major Ridge Home became a museum. Listed on the National Register of Historic Places, it is now a national landmark and designated sight along the Trail of Tears Designated Historic Trail. Visitors to the museum today experience exhibits, educational programs, and special events pertaining to Cherokee history and culture. However, there is another side to the museum that visitors may not be aware of. The Chieftains has a few unseen residents who still call this beautiful manor home.

Major Ridge's daughter, Nancy, died here in childbirth when she was only seventeen. The marks made from her fingernails as she clawed the walls in anguish during the torturous birth can still be seen on the upstairs wall today. The marks have been painted over numerous times, but they still remain. Six months after Nancy's death, her child perished also. There have been numerous reports of a baby crying at the museum. When the home was still a private residence, one former resident, a teen at the time, remembers playing records constantly to drown out the pitiful cries. Similarly, a collections manager in later years played CDs to mask the crying sounds. Debby Brown, a former museum employee, remembered searching both inside and outside the museum for the source of the crying sounds.

Another well-known ghost in the Chieftains is Nancy, herself. Her footsteps are often heard as she walks up and down the staircase and around the first and second floors. Paranormal investigators have captured what is believed to be her image in the home as well as her voice on their recorders. According to those who have experienced her presence, she is a friendly ghost—more curious than frightening. Perhaps she remains behind to be near her child. People have reported seeing a woman dressed in a white gown moving about in the museum. Passersby have reported seeing someone gazing down from the second-story windows of the museum when the museum is closed.

Nancy isn't perceived by museum employees as being a scary ghost. She has actually been known to be quite helpful. Debby once asked her daughter, Mollie, to turn out the lights at the museum. Mollie turned them out. A moment later, she asked Mollie to turn the lights on again. Before Mollie could reach the light switch, the lights turned on by themselves. "Thanks," Debby told Nancy. "I appreciate it."

According to Debby, her most unusual encounter with the ghosts of Chieftains involves the ghost of a small child that resides here. No one is sure who the child may be. Debby was preparing for a visit by a group of students from a local school. As part of their experience at the Chieftains, they were going to make wooden horse magnets on which they would write the Cherokee word for horse. Debby had spent the day painting over 120 wooden horses in preparation for the event. She had laid them out in the kitchen to dry. "Like little brown cookies," Debby said, the horses covered every surface in the kitchen, including the tops of the refrigerator and microwave. Debby was the last employee to leave that day, locking up the museum and leaving the wooden horses to dry in neat little rows.

That evening, her daughter, Mollie, remembered something she had left behind at the museum and needed for school the next day. Not exactly relishing the idea of being in the museum at night, Debby told her daughter they would stop by the museum on the way to school in the morning.

They arrived at the chieftains about forty-five minutes earlier than Debby's normal arrival time. Debby typed in the security code and the two entered the museum, deep in conversation about their plans for the day. Mollie led the way as they turned the corner in the hallway leading to the kitchen. Suddenly, she stopped, turned abruptly and began yelling, "Get out! Get out!" as she pushed her mother back down the hallway. They stumbled and fled back down the hallway toward the gift shop, Debby dumbfounded and Mollie shouting. Finally, in the gift shop, Mollie told her mother breathlessly, "We can't go in there! We can't!"

"But what did you see?" Debby asked.

Mollie stared at her mother in wonder. "Something . . . was playing with your horses!"

In the past Debby had avoided the strange noises and footsteps in the museum. This time, she had to see it for herself. "I'm going to see." She turned and headed back down the hallway.

"Don't go! Don't go back in there!" Mollie held tightly to Debby's arm as she resolutely marched back toward the kitchen and whatever it was her daughter had seen. Arriving in the kitchen, she found all the little brown horses lying in rows exactly as she had left them—except for two. One horse was lying upside down on top of another horse. One was lying at an angle on top of two other horses. Debby had been the last person to leave the museum the night before, setting the alarm as she left. Mollie had not been out of her sight that morning. Yet, here were two horses that had clearly been moved.

"What did you see?' she asked Mollie. "Tell me what did this."

"I don't know!" Mollie explained. "They were just moving in the air like this." She moved her hands up and down much like a child would do making horses move about.

"And there they were," explains Debby. "They were lying there just as if someone had been startled and dropped them." To this day, she has never found an explanation. Was a ghost child playing with the horses?

A paranormal investigative team was sitting in a circle one night in what had once been a bedroom in the home. One investigator said, "If you are here, hold my hand." The investigator then felt something similar to a cold water balloon resting in his hand.

Who is the mysterious child that haunts the Chieftains? Was he a member of the Ridge family? Did he live there in later years? Maybe his family worked on the farm or lived nearby.

The most recent ghost to be discovered at the Chieftains made his presence known during another school visit. A group of students had their picture made with a digital camera. When they looked at the picture, a man could be seen standing in back of the group in a corner. "Who is that?" the students wanted to know.

"We enlarged the picture," says Debby, "and there he was." A man's face was plainly visible in the corner. Debby does know of one man being murdered at the trading post that once stood just upriver from the house. Could it be the ghost of the murdered man still roaming the grounds? Or, perhaps, Major Ridge himself could be returning for a visit.

The Chieftains is open to the public Wednesday through Saturday from 10:00 a.m. until 5:00 p.m. You can visit their website at www.chieftainsmuseum.org.

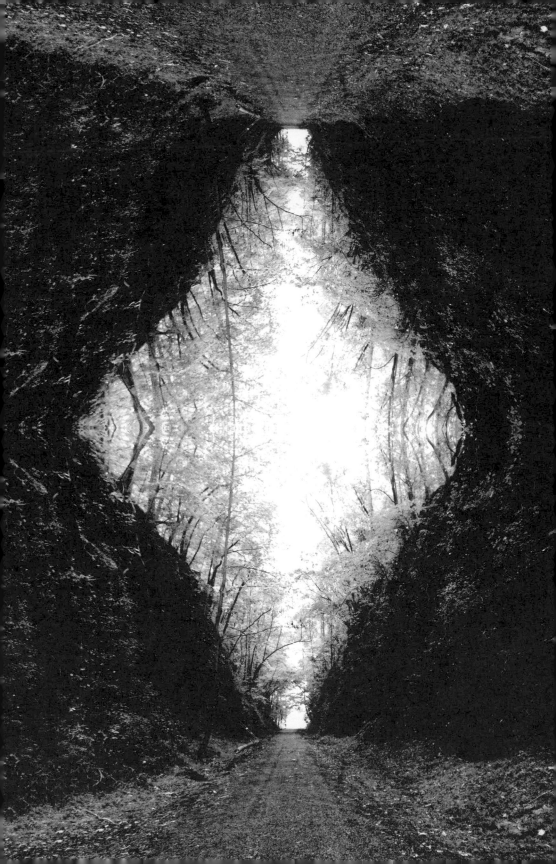

CHAPTER TWO

BARTOW COUNTY

Allatoona Pass
Emerson, GA

Allatoona Battlefield sits just off I-75, about forty-five minutes north of Atlanta. Now a part of Red Top Mountain State Park, the battlefield was the site of the Battle of Allatoona Pass on October 5, 1864. One of the most notable structures of the park is Deep Cut. Reaching more than 170 feet high and 95 feet long, Deep Cut was dug through the Allatoona Mountains to create a way for trains on the Western and Atlantic Railroad to get to Tennessee. General Tecumseh Sherman was so impressed with the structure when he passed through on his way to Marietta, that he avoided it during the Atlanta Campaign.

The battlefield offers a peaceful journey back in time to its visitors. It provides a lesson in history as well as beautiful scenery. However, if you choose to wander in this idyllic area that meanders peacefully along the shores of Lake Allatoona, you just may get more than you bargained for.

The first ghostly reports in the area began to surface in 1872. At the time, railroad workers on the W & A Railroad noticed that when they passed back and forth between Allatoona Pass and Tilton, Georgia, an extra brakeman appeared on their trains. He would appear on top of the freight cars and remain seated there for many miles before disappearing. When anyone approached him, he would vanish. This ghost became quite a sensation, and the story was carried in various papers throughout the south. This went on for quite some time.

Deep Cut, c. 2015. Courtesy of
David Jefferson Davis Jr.

Finally, an engineer on the W & A decided to settle the matter once and for all. One evening when the mysterious brakeman made his appearance, the determined engineer made his way along the cars to where the ghost sat. The ghost turned to watch the engineer approach. Just as the engineer was within distance to question the ghost, the ghost slowly faded from view. The engineer walked right through where the ghost had been sitting. He looked all around for a place a man could hide. Finding nothing, he turned back around to the way he had come. There was the mysterious brakeman again sitting exactly where he had been! Although many tried, no one was ever able to talk with the mysterious ghost. His reasons for appearing and disappearing on the train have been speculated for decades.

Trains no longer pass through Deep Cut. It is now a hiking trail. However, the whistles from passing trains can be heard nearby. Does the mysterious brakeman still ride with them?

It was the W&A Railroad that delivered the body of a soldier to Allatoona Station a few days after the Battle of Allatoona. Wearing a grey Confederate uniform and having a black broad-brimmed hat rolled up

The tracks have long been removed from Allatoona Pass, yet trains are often heard passing through here late at night. A piece of the old track remains today as a reminder of the trains that once passed through this small village each day, c. 2015 *Courtesy of David Jefferson Davis Jr.*

The Tomb of the Unknown Hero of Allatoona Pass, c. 2015 *Courtesy of David Jefferson Davis Jr.*

in his casket, the body carried no identification and his destination read only "Allatoona, Ga." No one claimed the body. After two days and two nights of lying in the Allatoona Station, he was buried by four local ladies. In 1880, a group of surveyors found the body and erected his tombstone. Known only as the Unknown Hero, he remains to this day, another great mystery of Allatoona Pass. Visitors report seeing mysterious lights near the grave and a few have even seen the shadowy figure of a man. Could it be the unknown hero? Perhaps he is still trying to make his way home.

Allatoona Pass is now a popular site for tourists and history buffs as well as ghost hunters. If what they say is true, very few leave disappointed. Many report the smell of gunpowder as well as orbs, mysterious lights, drops in temperature, and mysterious voices.

Allatoona Pass is on Old Allatoona Road in Emerson, Georgia. Take Exit 283 off I-75 and travel east for 1.5 miles.

CHAPTER THREE

CHATTOOGA COUNTY

A Nice House in the Country
Rural Area

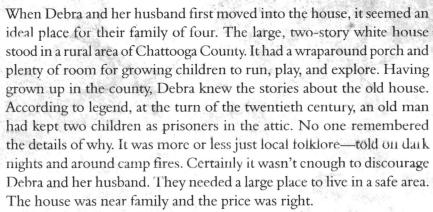

When Debra and her husband first moved into the house, it seemed an ideal place for their family of four. The large, two-story white house stood in a rural area of Chattooga County. It had a wraparound porch and plenty of room for growing children to run, play, and explore. Having grown up in the county, Debra knew the stories about the old house. According to legend, at the turn of the twentieth century, an old man had kept two children as prisoners in the attic. No one remembered the details of why. It was more or less just local folklore—told on dark nights and around camp fires. Certainly it wasn't enough to discourage Debra and her husband. They needed a large place to live in a safe area. The house was near family and the price was right.

Debra's Aunt Lisa had also lived in the house before Debra and her family moved in. One night Lisa had awakened from a deep sleep to find a man standing beside her bed. He was wearing an old-fashioned black suit and white shirt with a high, white collar. The man never turned to face Lisa, but instead cut his eyes toward her, watching her. She was paralyzed with fear. She never forgot that night, and moved from the house.

Even Lisa's experiences were not enough to discourage Debra and her family. They had a strong faith in God. They moved into the house and settled in.

From the very beginning, certain areas of the house gave Debra the creeps. There was an upstairs closet that contained the door to the attic. Debra never liked that closet and couldn't explain why. She just avoided it whenever possible.

Her daughter was two at the time. She spent her afternoons riding her tricycle around and around the wraparound porch. Sometimes she would stop her tricycle and stare across the road at a large tree that stood next to a small creek. As time passed and she got older, she began to point at the tree and say that she saw a little girl and boy there. Debra saw nothing and wrote it off to her daughter's imagination. "I would just say, 'Well, don't talk to them' or 'Don't play with them,' and go on about my business," she said. By the time her daughter had turned four, she stopped mentioning the girl and boy beside the tree. She never even looked over at the tree anymore.

One Wednesday night, the family was getting ready to go to church. Her four-year-old daughter told her there were bugs in her room. Debra went to investigate. The wall in her daughter's room was actually the back wall of the closet that held access to the attic. (On the other side of this wall was the closet.) Debra found maggots pouring out of a hole in the wall (from the closet). "The more I would sweep up, the more they came gushing out of that wall!" she remembers. Her husband told her there was probably something dead in the wall. Debra, however, felt that something worse was at play here. She immediately got out her Bible and began to read from Psalms, chapter 91:

> He that dwelleth in the secret place of the most high shall abide under the shadow of the Almighty. I will say of the Lord, He is my refuge and my fortress: my God; in Him I will trust. Surely, He shall deliver thee from the snare of the fowler and from the noisome pestilence.

She read the verse out loud over and over and prayed to God, telling Him she was trusting Him. The family then left the house to attend church. When they returned home, the maggots were gone. They couldn't even find a hole or crack where they had been.

Around the time Debra's younger child (a son) turned three, he started talking about his imaginary friends, Jimmy and Timmy. Debra knew that imaginary friends were common for children and thought little of it. Looking back, she now realizes that her son only played with his friends outside—never in the house.

One day, Debra went outside to call her son in to lunch. He told her he was busy playing with Jimmy and Timmy. She jokingly replied, "Well, you tell those two boys you've got to come in and eat!"

He replied, "No, Mama! Jimmy is a girl and Timmy is a boy!" Immediately, Debra got an eerie feeling. She remembered the boy and girl her daughter had seen across the road from the house. She told her son not to play with those children anymore.

Debra contacted her pastor and asked him to come and pray over the house. She felt that a house blessing would bring peace to it. Her son never mentioned the children again. Shortly after this, the family moved.

The house has since been torn down. Do the spirits of two lost children still wander the grounds of the old farm looking for playmates? If you find yourself traveling the backroads of Chattooga County and see a young boy and girl standing alone by a large tree . . . don't stop.

The Horse-Drawn Hearse
Near Trion

A curvy back road winds through a rural area of Chattooga County near the small town of Trion. As the road tops a hill, a small white country church appears. Behind the church, stretching to the woods beyond, lies an old cemetery flanked by a dirt road.

Dot's grandfather is buried in this cemetery, as well as a few of her other relatives. She and her sisters attended quite a few funerals in the church while they were growing up. Throughout those years, their grandmother would often tell them the story of the ghost hearse. According to local legend, a horse-drawn hearse could be heard coming up to the cemetery at night. Those who were brave enough to stay and watch could even see the specter as it rattled up the old dirt road into the cemetery. Once it entered the cemetery, it would disappear.

One night, Dot, her sisters, and some of their friends decided to test the story and see if it was true. They went to the graveyard late one night and waited. The church was abandoned at the time and the graveyard was unkempt. Grass grew tall among the stones. The church windows were dark, staring blankly into the night. According to Dot, it looked like no one even cared about the old church and cemetery anymore. It looked lonely and forgotten.

As the clock slowly approached midnight, the cemetery took on a creepy feeling. Shadows darted here and there. Suddenly the group heard a sound, quiet at first, then louder. A clip-clopping sound of hooves came nearer and nearer the cemetery. As the hoofbeats came closer, wooden wheels could be heard squeaking along the gravel road. Try as they might, the group could see nothing in the darkness. They could only hear the sounds of the ancient hearse as it made its way into the old cemetery.

The frightened group stared in silent disbelief as the hearse made its way into the cemetery, then became silent. The darkness enshrouded the group. The only sound to be heard now was the wind blowing through the silent gravestones. Quietly the group left the cemetery. Although they had seen nothing, the sounds they heard were proof enough. Their grandmother's stories were true after all.

Many stories have circulated about the old church and cemetery through the years. Some say the cemetery is haunted by a hanging that took place there in the 1800s. Some have even claimed to see the hangman's noose swinging from a large tree in the cemetery.

Dot and her sister cannot vouch for the hangman's noose, but they can definitely say they have heard the old hearse as it slowly made its way into the cemetery that dark night.

If you visit the cemetery one quiet, lonely night, you might also hear the hearse. According to legend, fall and winter nights are the best nights to visit. And don't mind that rope hanging from the tree above your head. It, too, will disappear come sunrise.

Company's Coming
Holland, Georgia

In the early 1950s, Sherry Donahue's father bought a house on Highway 100 about halfway between Summerville and Holland, Georgia. Sherry was four years old at the time. They reached the house by a long driveway that wound through the countryside on past their house to another house farther on.

Soon after moving in, the family began to experience strange things. The family would be sitting in the living room when something that sounded like a huge limb would hit the side of the house on the outside living room wall. There were no trees or bushes near that side of the house. The family would investigate, but find nothing amiss.

Often, the family would hear a car coming up the driveway. The car would stop in front of the house. Sometimes, one door could be heard opening and slamming shut. Sometimes, there would be two. Footsteps would walk up the front steps and across the wooden porch to the front door. Next, the family would hear a knock at the door. When the door was opened, no one would be there. This happened over and over, both during the day and at night.

One day, the family heard a car coming up the driveway, heard the door open and shut, and heard the steps walk up to the door. Sherry's mother turned to her daughters, rolled her eyes, and said, "I'm sure it's just our ghost." She went to the door, opened it up, and screamed loudly. It wasn't a ghost at the door, but a Watkin's salesman. According to Sherry, "My mother tried to explain. I'm sure he thought she was crazy. But that didn't stop him from coming back."

The house had a large wooden porch that extended across the back and down the side away from the driveway. The house had a small side room that opened onto this porch by a screen door. Footsteps would often walk down the porch toward the room. The screen door would rattle as if someone were trying to open it. When anyone went to the door, no one was there.

The family got used to the strange sounds, and went about life as normal. However, visitors were often frightened. On many occasions, the family would be entertaining company when a car could be heard coming down the driveway. As always, the car doors would open and shut; then the familiar footsteps would walk up to the door and knock. "You have company!" the visitors would tell them. Sherry or one of her family members would nonchalantly open the door and say, "No, it's just our ghost. See?" Often the visitors would be so frightened that they would not return. One neighbor refused to ever visit the house again, insisting the family come to his house instead.

There were rumors that a very mean family had once lived in the house. There was a great deal of feuding among the family members and even rumors of one family member killing another, then burying them in the woods nearby the house. The death had never been reported to authorities. Could this be the cause of the haunting? Maybe the murder victim is trying to return home.

A short time ago, Sherry went by the house to see if it was still standing. Indeed, it was still there. She wondered whether the family living there now still heard the steps of the mysterious visitor. The neighbor living in the house behind Sherry's old house had bought it years ago and rented it out until he'd finally sold it years later. Still she wonders about the current inhabitants. Are they ever sitting in the living room at night when a car pulls up in the drive and someone unseen knocks on the door?

Ola Mae
Summerville, GA

It was 1983 when Greg and Cassandra Thomas moved into the house in West Summerville with their two sons. The house had originally been built in 1927, but had undergone a couple renovations and additions. There was plenty of room for a growing family of four.

For the first six months, all was quiet and peaceful. Slowly, over time, however, the family began to notice odd noises here and there. It was never scary, just strange. Dishes would rattle when no one was in the kitchen. There were just odd noises that couldn't be written off to an old house settling. As the noises increased, so did other odd incidents.

A few times a month the Thomas's would wake up in the mornings and walk into their living room to find their recliner opened up into the reclining position. The first few times, they wondered if they had left it open. Not really giving it much thought, they'd set the recliner back into its original position and thought no more of it. A few days later, they would awaken to find it open again. After this became a regular occurrence, they began to wonder if something strange was at play.

One night, as his wife lay sleeping quietly beside him, Greg awoke with a start. A small woman was standing at the foot of the bed staring at him. She was slim and short in stature with white hair—a very tiny woman. She stared at him silently, then turned, walked out the bedroom door, and disappeared. Greg jumped up out of bed and followed the woman, but he could find no trace of her. After checking on the boys, he searched the entire house. He could find no trace of the mysterious woman.

Cassandra collected clown figurines. She displayed them on a small table in the living room. Sometimes, the Thomases would get up in the morning and find all the clown figurines turned toward the wall. Greg tried to find an explanation. He even stood in front of the table and jumped up and down. "I just wanted to see if maybe our walking by was causing it to happen," he said. "I couldn't even get them to move."

However, it kept happening. The clowns would be facing out into the living room when the Thomases went to bed, and they'd awaken to find them facing the wall. This continued for years and no explanation was ever found. Greg was never able to catch the clowns in movement, and was never able to make them move.

Shortly after receiving his driver's license, Greg's youngest son left the house one day. As he drove around the house, he saw an older woman sitting on the swing. She was small in stature with white hair. He did a double take, and she was gone.

A short time later, he was coming home from school and saw an older woman sitting on the front steps. Thinking his grandmother had come for a visit, he parked his car and walked around the house to say hello. When he got there, the steps were empty. No one was there. Bewildered, he walked into the house. His grandmother was not there and had not been there at all that day.

When Greg and Cassandra retired at night, they'd often talk awhile before going to sleep. Eventually, they'd turn out the light and start to drift off. It was during this time between wakefulness and sleep that they'd feel it. It felt exactly as if someone were sitting down on the bed with them. They'd both feel it and look at the same time. No one was there. They'd reach toward what they felt—but nothing was there.

Finally, Greg contacted the woman who had sold him the house. He had to have some answers. She didn't seem surprised when he asked if someone had ever died in the house. Yes, she told him, the previous owner, a woman by the name of Ola Mae, had died in the house. She had died in her bedroom—where his living room was now. When he asked her to describe Ola Mae, she described the same woman he and his son had seen: a small elderly woman, short and slim, with white hair.

After that, when strange noises would begin in the house, the family members would shout. "That's enough Ola Mae!" and the noises would stop.

One night, Greg and Cassandra were in the living room when they heard the dishes in the kitchen rattling. As the noise became louder, they both got up to investigate. When they entered the kitchen, they were met with silence. Nothing was amiss. Bewildered, they left the kitchen and headed into the dining room. They hadn't taken one step out of the kitchen into the dining room when the dishes began to rattle again. Eventually, the rattling dishes became another common noise in the house. "We'd just say, Miss Ola Mae, be quiet!" he said. "And she'd stop. We were never scared. It was always a loving feeling. It never felt angry."

One day, Greg's friend, a boss at a nearby mill, passed Greg's house after work. "I saw your mom at your house today," he told Greg.

"No," Greg told him. "You didn't see my mom. She wasn't at the house today."

"Yes, she was!" he replied. "I saw her sitting on your steps!"

"What did she look like?" Greg asked.

"She was a little woman with white hair," his friend replied.

"That wasn't my mom," Greg told him.

Eventually, sightings of Ola Mae became less and less. Greg's wife, Cassandra, passed away after a fight with cancer. Shortly after her death, Greg could feel Cassandra's presence throughout the home. When he retired at night, he could feel Cassandra nearby. It was as if she was making sure he was okay and saying goodbye.

As time went on, Greg began to feel the presence of Cassandra and Ola Mae less and less. Now, he does not feel the presence of Cassandra or Ola Mae any more. He still resides in the house. Perhaps Ola and Cassandra have moved on and are at peace.

The Man in the Tan Coat
Summerville, GA

A short time after Sandy moved into the house on Fish Hatchery Road in Chattooga County, she was out in the yard at her dog pen when she heard someone loudly whisper her name. It scared her so badly that she quickly ran into the house. After that, strange things began to happen on a regular basis. Her bedroom light would come on during the night by itself. She, her husband, and their three children were all in bed asleep. No one could have turned on the light. Still, it would come on and wake her up regularly.

Soon after, Sandy started seeing a man wearing a tan coat outside her house. She would get a glimpse of him walking by her kitchen window. When she went outside to see who could be walking in her yard, no one was there. One afternoon, Sandy and her oldest daughter were sitting at the kitchen table. "Mom," her daughter told her, "there is someone coming to your back door." She got up and went to the door, but no one was there. She went out onto the carport, but found no one. Returning to the kitchen, she asked her daughter if the man had been wearing a tan coat. Her daughter replied. "Yes!" Until that time, she had never told her children about the man in the tan coat. As it turns out, her husband had also seen the man in the tan coat near the dog pen.

Behind the house was a small lake, and across the lake was an older house that was being remodeled at the time. On several nights, Sandy and her husband saw a light on at the house across the lake. Later, when she mentioned this to the lady remodeling the house, the lady informed her that the house had no electricity. There couldn't have possibly been a light at the house. Later on, Sandy and her husband would see lights moving around between their house and the house across the lake. They never found a source for the lights or an explanation.

However strange her experiences may have been, Sandy never felt threatened by the spirit. Actually, she felt protected. When she went through a divorce later on, she felt that the spirit was watching over her and protecting her. The spirit felt more like a watchful friend.

When she moved from the house, she sold it to her brother. She asked her brother if he had ever seen the man in the tan coat or had any paranormal experiences. He had never seen anything unusual. Maybe the spirit knew that Sandy and her family were okay and had therefore, finally found rest.

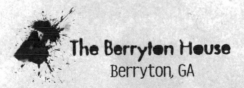

The Berryton House
Berryton, GA

Berryton Georgia is primarily a mill village that grew up around the old Harriet and Henderson Cotton Mill. The houses were originally built by the cotton mill for workers. Churches and even schools were built and added to the community. However, the hub of the community remained the cotton mill. Generations of families grew up in this village and called Berryton home.

Khevin grew up in one of these houses. Years before, a little girl had been scalded to death in what became Khevin's bedroom. Details to the tragedy had been lost in time, but the stories remained, passed down through generations. Along with the stories, strange occurrences plagued the family—incidences that couldn't be explained.

One evening, as Khevin sat in his bedroom, a stack of books on a shelf actually levitated into the air and then dropped to the floor. Terrified, Khevin ran from the room, almost knocking his mom down in his haste to escape.

Once a neighbor was visiting the house and was burned by a candelabra. However, the candelabra had not been lit in many years. Wanting to rid the house of the thing, Khevin took the candelabra out of the house and down to the creek. He still remembers how it felt very warm to his touch. How could a candelabra that hadn't been lit for years inflict a burn?

On two different occasions, Khevin's uncles visited the home. Both were awakened during the night by an old woman standing at the foot of the bed and informing them in a terse voice, "I guess you know that this is MY house."

One day, a perfect profile of a head appeared on the wall of Khevin's bedroom. The family attempted to paint over the profile several times, but it remained for many years. No one ever found an explanation for the oddity.

When the family was renovating the house, they found two hidden rooms that they had never known existed! Khevin made one of the rooms his new bedroom, leaving his old room to become a den. Underneath the floor in this room he found a hidden crawlspace. Was this a place where a family hid their treasured belongings? Was this house once a part of the underground railroad?

When family was tearing out an old wall, they found a young girl's shoe hidden inside the wall. Did it belong to the girl who had died so tragically in the room years before? Although she never appeared to Khevin in all his years in the house, she did appear to other family members. Her burns were visible to those who saw her. Khevin's mom still has the mysterious little shoe.

Another item found in the wall was an old knife, the blade rusted and covered with what appeared to be dried blood. It was a large knife and was wedged into the wall of the kitchen pantry. No explanation for the knife was ever found.

In December 1980, Khevin's grandmother (who also lived in the house) passed away. The pantry had always been her domain. She

Khevin's family found a young girl's shoe hidden inside a wall of their house when they were renovating. Did it belong to the young girl who died there? c. 2015. *Courtesy of Khevin Farmer.*

loved to can and preserve vegetables (like most southern women of her generation). She stored them in the pantry. A few months after her death, white crosses mysteriously appeared on each of her jars. Khevin and his family took this as a sign that she was at peace.

Although Khevin has since moved from the house in Berryton, he has never forgotten his experiences growing up in a haunted house. A few years ago, the old house burned to the ground. Only the old shoe remains as a testament to the secrets the old house held.

The Child in the Fog
Chattoogaville, GA

It was a balmy Saturday night, around midnight, as a young couple made their way along Price Bridge Road in the Holland-Chattoogaville area of Chattooga County. It had rained earlier and mists of steam rose up from the road. Fog hung like a damp curtain, making the car's headlights all but useless. It was prom night and the couple was tired from all the excitement.

The girl lay her head on her boyfriend's shoulder and was just beginning to drift off, when he suddenly hit the brakes. Her eyes flew open as the car came to a screeching halt. The couple stared in disbelief at what stood in the road just in front of them. A small child, around two years old, stood in front of the car staring intently at the couple. Wearing only a diaper, the toddler stood on bare feet all alone in the fog.

"A baby!" the girl exclaimed! Neither of the teenagers recognized the toddler, but both assumed it must belong to a home nearby. Maybe it had somehow walked out of the house while the parents were sleeping. In these days before cell phones, the couple decided to try and talk to the baby and hopefully get it into the car with them so they could take it to safety.

Slowly, they got out of the car and began to approach the child, who remained stark still in the roadway watching the couple warily.

"Hey, sweet baby!" the girl cooed. "Are you lost?"

Suddenly, the baby turned toward the side of the road, took a couple steps into the mist and disappeared! The shocked couple ran after the baby and began searching frantically. However, the baby was gone. It had vanished into thin air.

The frightened couple clambered back into the car and raced to a nearby farmhouse. A light was on in one window and they ran onto the porch hoping someone was awake (and would not shoot them) this late at night.

An older man came to the door and listened calmly and quietly to the story. Finally, he just shook his head. "Don't worry about that baby," he said. "Go on home and get some rest."

"We can't just leave it out there!" the boy exclaimed. "We have to find it!"

"You won't find that baby," the man replied. "That baby ain't real. I don't know what he is…but he ain't of this world. I can tell you that. You ain't the first one to see him."

The stunned couple made their way back to the car and drove to the girl's house in disbelief. The girl's parents were not surprised to

Price Bridge Cemetery
c. 2015.

Does the mysterious child roaming Price Bridge Road come from this cemetery or from one of the farmhouses nearby? c. 2015

hear about the mysterious child, as it turned out. They agreed that the child was not of this world.

Although neither the boy or girl ever saw the child again, they never forgot the night that the child stood staring at them from the misty country road.

Many people have encountered the child as they drive along this quiet road, particularly on warm nights after a rain. Does the child come from a nearby cemetery? Did it live in one of the homes nearby?

Chatoogaville is rich in history. Home to some of the first settlers in the county, there are many historic homes and cemeteries here. Legends abound in the area, many of which center around the Johnson family. Jeff Johnson Sr. was once known as "the meanest man in Chattooga County." Many of his sons (and a son-in-law) met their end on the end of a rope for their crimes.

One of Jeff's sons, Gus, was rumored to have killed a baby and chopped it into pieces. This happened in the late 1860s or early 1870s, and Gus was hanged in Floyd County in 1878. He was not hanged for the murder of a baby, however. He was hanged for murdering an older African American man who drove a ferry that crossed the Chattooga River in Holland. Some say the ferry man was not moving fast enough. Some say Gus just got his feet wet. Both Jeff and Gus are buried in the Chattoogaville area, but in different cemeteries.

Although no one knows the exact origin of the child that roams the roads of the Holland-Chattoogaville area on rainy summer nights, few dispute the fact that the child exists. It remains a part of the local lore, an unsolved mystery from the distant past.

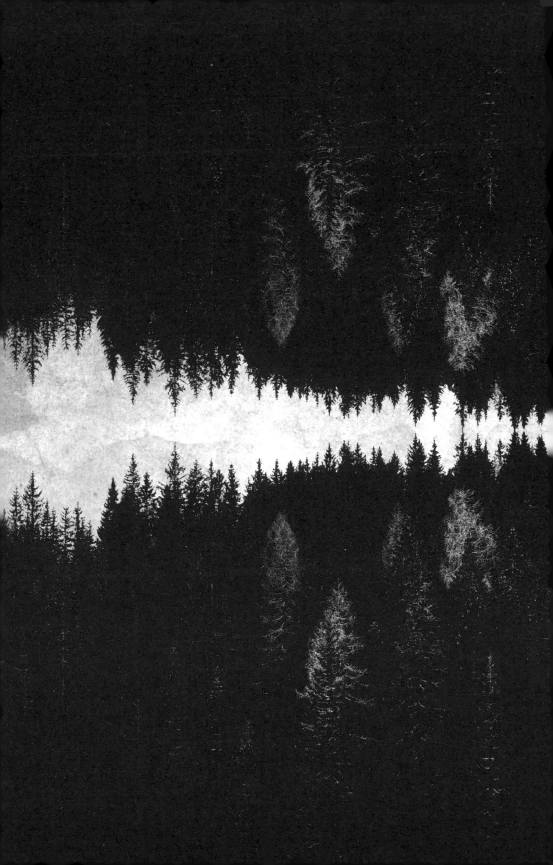

CHAPTER FOUR

WHITFIELD COUNTY

The Blue Hole
Varnell, GA

A disappearing, but very important, part of Northwest Georgia's past was the Great Federal Road, which was once the only route for passengers traveling through Cherokee Territory from Augusta to Nashville.

Before the white man entered Northwest Georgia, the community of present-day Varnell was known as Red Hill, named for the red clay hills surrounding the settlement. Home to about a dozen Cherokee families, Red Hill was located on what was known as the Middle Cherokee Trading Path. Later renamed the Georgia Road in the 1790s, the state made this route a path for settlers traveling through Cherokee lands on their way to the Tennessee River. In 1803, the federal government began to take interest in the Georgia Road as a route from Southeast Georgia into Nashville. In the Treaty of Tellico in 1805, the Cherokee ceded valuable lands for the creation of this new roadway, and the Great Federal Road was born.

In some areas, the Federal Road was an actual dirt road, winding through the Georgia countryside. In other areas, it became a mere path at best, worn over time by horses, wagons, and foot travelers. Farmers, planters, slaves, mail carriers, and Indian negotiators all used the Federal Road. Travel along the route could be treacherous and downright dangerous as travelers passed through stretches of lonely countryside. The taverns, inns, and stores located along the route became welcome respites.

A regular stagecoach route was established along this route in the 1820s. It is the tragic story of a lonely stagecoach traveling the Federal Road that still haunts the tiny community of Varnell today.

It was a dark, cold, and stormy night near Christmas in the early 1830s. A lone stagecoach was making its way south from Ringgold toward the settlement at Red Hill. Surrounded by darkness, the coach rattled along in drenching rains and terrible cold. The driver couldn't see his hand in front of his own face. The only light would have been from the occasional lightning as it ripped across the sky. Relying on the horses, who knew this path well, the driver bent his head against the rain and hoped to reach the safety of Red Hill soon. How many times did the coach become mired in the mud and muck caused by the torrential rains? One can only imagine the misery of man and beast alike as they crept through Cherokee territory hoping to find shelter ahead.

When the horses suddenly came to a stop, refusing to move any farther, both driver and crew were surely overwhelmed with frustration. The poor animals must have sensed the danger that lay just ahead. Eager to be near civilization with a good drink and warm, dry shelter, the tired driver whipped the animals and urged them on. The two horses in front most likely balked and tried to back away from what they sensed lay ahead. As nervous, exasperated passengers began to complain, the driver began to whip the horses nearest him even harder, causing them to push the front horses forward against their will. The stagecoach clattered on.

Imagine, if you will, what it was like to be a passenger on this stagecoach on that horrible night. The passengers, unused to the discomforts of being stranded in a raging winter thunderstorm, were sore and tired from the constant jostling about on the rough road. The ladies were likely crying and praying to reach Red Hill soon. Surely the gentlemen tried their best to comfort the ladies, although they, too, longed for the relative safety of the settlement at Red Hill. Matters were made worse by the utter darkness. The passengers couldn't see the person sitting next to them. This is what was likely taking place inside the coach as the driver struggled with the horses up front.

What happened next is a matter of speculation. For over a century the citizens of Varnell have tried to piece it together. Such a horror is hard to conceive.

Suddenly, the coach must have surged forward. The horses in front would have been unable to stop, pushed on by those behind being whipped into a frenzy by the driver. What happened next probably took only minutes, but must have seemed like hours. Passengers were likely flung into one another or even out of the coach as it tumbled forward and down, down, into utter darkness. Imagine, if you will, the terror of then being surrounded and covered by icy water that could not be seen.

Imagine the terror of wondering what was happening as cries of animal and human alike tore through the night, as bodies were tossed about in the darkness before sinking quickly into unseen icy water.

The next morning, residents of Red Hill became concerned for the stagecoach that never arrived. A search party was formed and headed out through the mud and bitter cold. As the group trudged through the woodlands and started down a hill they were caught up short. Ahead of them in the middle of the road was a body of water that had not existed the day before. The mysterious pond was about 75 feet in diameter. Where had it come from?

Making their way slowly through the mud, the searchers edged their way around to the other side of the pond where the roadway began again. There, to their horror, they found hoofprints and the tracks of the stagecoach going straight into the pond. Nearby, one member of the search party found a bloody whip lying on the ground. Another found a lady's bonnet covered in mud lying near the water's edge. This is all that remained of passengers, driver, and horses. They were somewhere beneath the surface of the deep dark water, never to be seen again.

Shortly after the incident, travelers along the Federal Road began to experience strange happenings near the Blue Hole, as it later came to be called. Some claimed to see a headless man standing near the murky water. Was he a victim of the tragedy? Did he somehow lose his head in the bedlam as the stagecoach tumbled into the hole?

In the late 1800s, a woman ran breathlessly to the house of a friend in Varnell Station (the name had changed by then) and fainted at her door. When revived, she told of walking the Federal Road near the Blue Hole when suddenly an invisible horse rushed upon her. She could hear the beast, but could not see it. She could feel its hot breath against the back of her neck as she ran. To this day, many people have heard the thunder of unseen hooves and felt the breath of an unseen horse near the Blue Hole.

Perhaps the most famous tale surrounding the Blue Hole is of the stagecoach itself. On dark nights near Christmas, witnesses have heard the thunder of hooves and the clattering and squeaking of the old coach as it rumbled by on the Federal Road and tumbled over into the darkness of the Blue Hole. Is this a residual haunting caused by the imprint of such a horrifying event?

The Blue Hole sits on private property in a wooded area in the community of Varnell, Georgia. It cannot be reached without permission of the property owner.

CHAPTER FIVE

GORDON COUNTY

Resaca Confederate Cemetery
- Resaca, GA

On May 14 and 15, 1864, the first battle of the Atlanta Campaign was fought in Resaca, Georgia. In two days' time, more than 11,000 men from both the Union and Confederate armies lost their lives.

When Mary Green and her family returned to their plantation after the battle, they were met by a gruesome sight. The lawn surrounding their house was filled with the shallow graves of soldiers who had been buried where they fell. At that time, Mary and her sister, Pyatt, decided to build a cemetery for these men—a place consecrated to their memory.

Resaca Confederate Cemetery, c 2015.

Mary's father donated two-and-a-half acres of his land to the cause, a quiet, wooded area surrounding a small stream.

Having no money with which to build the cemetery, Mary started a letter-writing campaign, sending letters to friends and acquaintances throughout the state. Times were hard, and most could only send a nickel or dime to the cause. Her campaign began in July 1866, and was finished in October that same year. By December, all debts on the project had been paid.

It was Mary and Pyatt, along with their cook and maid, who began the task of digging up the bodies of the fallen and entering them into their new place of quiet rest. More than 450 men were buried in the cemetery.

The Resaca Cemetery and another Confederate cemetery in Winchester, Virginia, were consecrated and dedicated on the same day, each thinking theirs was the first.

Resaca Cemetery sits at the end of a deadend road in a quiet neighborhood. A small bridge spans a brook running through the wooded area. During the day, visitors to the area are immediately captivated by the peaceful, idyllic setting. At night, however, the atmosphere changes drastically. Strange lights and shadows dart here and there. Visitors have been touched by unseen hands. A few have even been grabbed around their ankles when standing near the brook.

Southern States Paranormal (http://southernstatespara.wix.com/ssp1) has done several investigations in the cemetery. They often use it to train new recruits, since they are almost guaranteed to get evidence. Along with many photos of orbs and vortexes, they have also captured the image of a soldier crouched beside a tree and a horse rearing up on its back legs.

Resaca Confederate Cemetery c. 2015.

Mary Green raised the funds for Resaca Confederate Cemetery and personally helped to enter the fallen soldiers' bodies into their final resting place, c. 2014.

Adam Dean and Matt Wnorowski of Southern States Paranormal recall being on the far side of the cemetery when they noticed the figure of a soldier slowly walking back and forth with his gun on his shoulder near the cemetery gate. They tried to approach the ghostly sentry, but he disappeared when they got close. However, once they were on the other side of the gate, they could see that the soldier again was walking back and forth guarding the gate.

The investigative team has also seen figures marching back and forth along the top of the hill that rises along one side of the cemetery. The figures made no sound as they silently walked back and forth. The investigators noted that they couldn't help but wonder if the people residing in the houses near the cemetery experienced any activity.

Another ghost said to haunt the cemetery is that of a little girl. She wears a white dress similar to those worn around the turn of the twentieth century. Some have seen her peeking out from behind a large tree in a far corner of the cemetery. Who could she be? Some say she is a child who lived on the plantation when the Greens were burying the soldiers. No one will ever know for sure. It does seem strange, a young girl ghost in a cemetery where no children are buried.

Resaca Confederate Cemetery is located near Interstate 75 in Resaca, Georgia. It is open to the public year-round. Because of its remote location, this is not a place to visit alone. Many unsavory events of the non-supernatural kind have occurred here. Be sure to visit with a small group and, as always treat the area with respect and leave it as you found it.

CHAPTER SIX

CATOOSA COUNTY

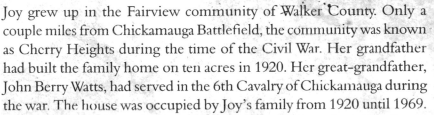

The Soldiers
Chickamauga, GA

Joy grew up in the Fairview community of Walker County. Only a couple miles from Chickamauga Battlefield, the community was known as Cherry Heights during the time of the Civil War. Her grandfather had built the family home on ten acres in 1920. Her great-grandfather, John Berry Watts, had served in the 6th Cavalry of Chickamauga during the war. The house was occupied by Joy's family from 1920 until 1969.

When her mother, aunts, and uncles were children, they often found minni balls and other Civil War artifacts in the yard around the house. In 1966, Joy found the finial of a flagpole in the yard.

In the early 1960s, Joy lived in the house with her mother and grandmother. One day, when Joy was around five years old, she walked into the house for lunch and found five men sitting around her grandmother's kitchen table. They were talking, laughing, and enjoying their meal. Although none of her family was present, Joy felt no threat from the men. Her grandmother often had visitors, so it came as no surprise that these men were enjoying a meal in her grandmother's kitchen. She immediately recognized that these men were wearing military uniforms. She had seen pictures of her uncles in their World War II uniforms and was familiar with military attire. She did notice that the uniforms these men wore were rather tattered and quite different from her uncles' uniforms.

While little Joy took in the scene around the table, the soldiers turned to her. "Well hello, little girl!" one soldier exclaimed. "What is your name? Would you like to eat with us?" They were jovial, friendly, and seemed to genuinely enjoy the little girl's company. She walked over to the soldier and he took her onto his lap and offered her some food. She has no memory of what the soldiers were eating. She remembers little else of the conversation, except that the soldiers were very happy to have her company. She does remember that they were talking about being tired from battle and were grateful for the food. She assumed her mom and grandmother were elsewhere in the house and that these friendly men were friends of her Uncle Charley.

She doesn't remember how the lunch ended or how the soldiers left. When she later mentioned the soldiers to her mother and grandmother, they had no idea what she was talking about. They didn't know of any men in the house. They suggested that perhaps the little girl had been dreaming. However, Joy had been very much awake when she'd walked into the kitchen. She remembers her lunch with the soldiers until this very day.

A year or so later, Joy's mother took her to visit friends of the family on Lytle Road across the street from the Chickamauga Battlefield. This was about five miles from Joy's home. While her mother visited, Joy asked if she might go outside and look around. She was given permission to play outside, although she was given a specific area that was okay for playing and exploring.

Inside this area was a small building with no roof. It had a few floor joists, a dirt floor, and four walls, but the roof was no longer there. When Joy entered the old building, she saw several men sitting around the sides of the structure. At first, she recalls, they seemed to blend in with the rock walls. After a few minutes, she could see them clearly. They sat around the walls and even on the ground. As Joy entered, the men stopped their conversation and stared at her. Just as at her grandmother's, Joy felt no fear. She doesn't think they were the same men she had seen at her grandmother's house, but it is hard for her to remember for sure. She does recall that there were about eight men in all.

Although they introduced themselves to her, she does not remember their names. They asked who she was and why she happened to be there that day. They seemed very amused at her name—Joy—a name unfamiliar to them. Seeming glad to have her company, the friendly soldiers continued to talk among themselves and included Joy in their conversations. They laughed and joked with each other. Joy remembers their tattered gray uniforms and their knapsacks, canteens, and weapons lying about. Some were wearing hats; some were not. She knew they were soldiers, although, again not like her uncle. They told her they were just resting for a while. She does remember that they commented on how no one had been able to see them in quite a while.

Eventually, Joy heard her mother calling for her. She found her mother on the porch, a few feet from the building where Joy had been with the soldiers. She asked her mother to come with her and meet the funny men in the building. Her mother and the owners of the house were quite worried at the thought of strange men in their building. Quietly, they approached the building where Joy and the soldiers had talked and laughed just minutes before. However, when they entered the building, no one was there. The old building appeared to have been unoccupied for ages. Where laughter had been just moments before, silence sat thick among the cobwebs. None of the adults believed Joy's story. Although they halfheartedly searched for these strange men who had supposedly been in their building, no one actually believed the little girl had seen anyone—much less talked with them.

Joy was fifty-our years old at the telling of this story. She vividly remembers her visits with the soldiers as if it were yesterday. She maintains that she was not dreaming and really did have conversations with soldiers from the past.

DADE COUNTY

Guardian Ghost of the Canyon
Cloudland Canyon State Park
RISING FAWN, GA

Cloudland Canyon State Park sits on the western edge of Lookout Mountain in Rising Fawn, Georgia. Straddling a deep gorge cut into the mountain by Sitton Gulch Creek, the park is one of the largest state parks in Georgia. Since being designated a state park in 1938, the park has grown from private land donations to 3,485 acres. Noted for its remote, quiet atmosphere and scenic views, Cloudland Canyon is a popular destination for campers and day-hikers alike.

Cloudland Canyon State Park, c. 2015.

However, when night settles upon the park and even the latest of the night owl guests have turned in for the evening, a visitor of a different kind enters the park. The horse he rides walks slowly through the campground on silent feet. As he rides among the campsites, few campers are aware of his passing. Those lucky enough to catch a glimpse of him, though startled, are not afraid. They describe him as being dressed as a Native Indian brave. He seems to be watching over the visitors there and has come to be known as "the Guardian Ghost of Cloudland Canyon." He has also been seen at a point above the canyon watching visitors below. Early morning risers often find the footprints of an unshod horse throughout the campground.

Guests, however, are not all that he is guarding. The area that is now Cloudland Canyon was once the home of the Cherokee. They had a valuable lead mine here. Although they kept its location secret, they were glad to trade with the white settlers nearby who used the lead

A Cherokee Brave silently rides through this campground in Cloudland Canyon State Park at night, c. 2105.

Does the ghost of a Cherokee brave still guard a
secret lead mine hidden in Cloudland Canyon?
c. 2015. *Courtesy of David Jefferson Davis Jr.*

for bullets. When the Cherokee were removed on the famous Trail of
Tears, they took their secrets with them, never revealing the location
of the mine. Although many have searched, it has never been found.
Does this lone Cherokee brave still roam Cloudland Canyon guarding
the secret mine for his people?

   Plan a night of camping in the park. Bring your tent or camper, or
stay in one of the yurts or cottages that the park has to offer. When the
park becomes silent and most campers are fast asleep, stay awake. Sit
outside and listen quietly. If you wait patiently, you may get to meet the
Guardian of the Canyon.

CHAPTER EIGHT

JUST OVER THE LINE

(Northeast Alabama)

Ghosts of Chesterfield
Chesterfield, AL

Chesterfield, Alabama, is a rural area in a beautiful valley that stretches along the Jamestown Road between Menlo, Georgia, and Jamestown, Alabama. Chesterfield is a small community, and most people passing through don't even give the place a second thought. A few houses, rolling countryside . . . hardly the place one would expect a haunting. As it turns out, though, Chesterfield has more than one ghost.

The TAG (Tennessee, Alabama, and Georgia) Railway once ran through Chesterfield as it passed from Chattanooga, Tennessee, to Gadsden, Alabama. Originally the Chattanooga Southern Railway, its name was changed to the TAG Railway in 1922. The TAG was eventually dismantled, except for a small segment in Northwest Georgia. One of the most famous haunts in the area is a light that is often seen at night along the old TAG Railroad bed. Many a coon hunter has come upon the light unexpectedly. The light moves along the railroad path, then turns right, and heads up the ridge.

Everyone agrees on one thing: if you are searching for the light, you will never see it. Many thrill seekers have gone in search of the light, and it has never shown itself. That's the reason it is so often seen by coon hunters—they aren't searching for it but come upon it accidentally. One man remembers looking for the light several times and never seeing it, then seeing it by accident more than once. One coon hunter remembers seeing it in the 1980s, and it made his hair stand on end. Even during the day, the area holds an air of creepiness. No birds singing . . . the air is still and quiet. You feel as if someone is watching you.

Some say the light is a remnant from a long-ago train wreck. Some say it is from a far more sinister source. Legend has it that, in the 1800s. a local citizen was studying to become a doctor. He went to Chattanooga in search of a human cadaver to study. He brought the body back to Alabama, but various versions of the story speculate as to whether he brought back a body or an actual live human being. He may have purchased the cadaver from grave robbers, or others, who obtained bodies by more sinister means. He may have actually started out from Chattanooga with a live human. At some point, before or after the trip to Alabama, the person was killed and the bones were boiled down for study. This took place near the bend of the ridge where the light is most often sighted. According to legend, the light is the soul of the poor cadaver searching for his body.

Mandy Walker and her husband lived near the site of the old railroad bed in the 1990s. One night, near midnight, they were sitting outside enjoying the breeze when they heard the distinctive sound of a train whistle. They listened again, not believing their ears. The nearest train was over the mountain in Valley Head, several miles away. Sure enough, they heard it again. A train was blowing its whistle and traveling on the TAG along tracks that had been taken up long ago. They heard the train several times over the years. They named it the Ghost Train. Until they moved from the area, they often heard it on quiet nights, passing into the darkness toward a long ago destination.

Another story that takes place in the Chesterfield/ Jamestown area is the story of the lost regiment. During the Civil War, a small group of Union soldiers got separated from their regiment in a skirmish near Adamsburg and became lost. They were wounded and hungry. As they began to wander the area, loss of blood and lack of food caused them to become disoriented and desperate. One by one, they began to die. As locals became aware of the roaming band of soldiers, they became concerned for their own safety. They began shooting them on sight. Now the soldiers were not only starving and suffering from untended battle wounds, but also hiding in fear. The last reported sighting of the soldiers was near Blanche, Alabama, just down the Jamestown Road from Chesterfield. There appeared to be six or seven men remaining. They were headed up the mountain. No one ever saw them again—at least not alive.

The ghosts of the soldiers have been seen at many places along the mountain and in the valley. They appear frightened and are crying for help. Sometimes, men's voices will be heard cursing in the distance. Other times, their voices are heard wailing moaning in misery as they try to find their way to safety. On a few occasions, mysterious footprints are found in the fields. They appear to be made from men's boots. However, they seem to come from nowhere and disappear abruptly.

If you find yourself near Chesterfield, Alabama, on a quiet night, stop, look, and listen. You may be approached by a mysterious light. You might hear the whistle of a ghost train. You might even meet up with a small group of Union soldiers crying for help.

Granny Dollar and Buster
DeSoto Falls
MENTONE, AL

Nancy Emmaline Callahan was born around 1827 in Buck's Pocket, Alabama, the daughter of a Cherokee father and a half-Cherokee, half–Scots-Irish mother. Her father also had a wife and children in South Carolina, which he had been forced to leave behind when coming west. Since it was legal at that time for Cherokee men to have more than one wife, Nancy's mother insisted her father send for his family. Both families lived happily together in Alabama, and between both wives, Nancy's father had twenty-six children. Nine of these were three sets of triplets born to Nancy's mother.

Although Nancy's family sounds strange by today's standards, they were actually very happy. The children played Cherokee games and helped on the family farm. The family lived completely off the land, cooking their meals in a red clay oven beneath a shed in their yard.

When the Cherokee removal began, Nancy's family didn't want to leave their beloved home in Alabama. Instead of leaving, they moved into a cave and lived there in hiding. This was their home for a while, until Nancy's father got into an altercation with a white man. The family was finally forced to leave their beloved home. With heavy hearts, the moved to a new home in Marthasville, Georgia.

While living in Georgia, Nancy became engaged to be married. Her fiancé, Thomas Porter, was the son of a storekeeper. Sadly, Thomas was killed during the Civil War. After his death, Nancy remained single for the next forty years.

Finally, in her seventies, Nancy met and married Norman Dollar. The happy couple moved to Mentone, Alabama. For the next twenty years, Nancy and Norman lived happily in Mentone, along with a mongrel dog named Buster.

When Norman passed away, a heartbroken Nancy sold her only cow in order to buy a headstone for his grave. Nancy and Buster moved into a cabin owned by Colonel Milford Howard. Nancy was very special to Colonel Howard and he was a great deal of support to her during this time. Nancy also supported herself by raising chickens and vegetables and by telling fortunes. Nancy and Buster were a common sight in the Mentone area as they walked along the road near DeSoto Falls, or sat on the steps of their cabin. Although Nancy was much loved by the citizens of Mentone, Buster was another story. His love and devotion to Nancy were undoubted. However, to others he was a grouchy, mean dog. He had bitten more than a few people in the area. Nancy's neighbors despised him.

Finally, in January 1931, Nancy passed away. She was 105 years old. Her beloved Buster was twenty. Nancy had saved $23 for her own headstone. Shortly after her death, someone stole the money, so Nancy's grave had no headstone.

Buster grieved deeply over the death of his mistress. Neighbors tried to feed him and take him in, but he refused. Instead, he remained at the door of Nancy's cabin, gnawing at the door and trying to get in. He was slowly starving to death. When it became obvious the dog was slowly dying an agonizing death, compassionate neighbors put him to death. Some sources say he was chloroformed, although it is questionable as to who would have been able to get that close to him. Buster was given his own funeral with Colonel Milford delivering the eulogy. Buster was laid to death at the base of a large boulder at what is now the Alpine Camp for Boys.

Shortly after their deaths, many people saw Granny Dollar and Buster walking the road near their cabin and around the DeSoto Falls

Do the spirits of Granny Dollar and Buster still roam the area near DeSoto Falls? c. 2015.

area. Others saw her sitting with Buster on the steps of their cabin. Still others heard her calling for Buster when they passed near her cabin.

For over forty years, sightings of the pair became quite common in the area. Locals speculated that Nancy could not rest because the money for her headstone had been stolen. She was awaiting justice. In 1973, the citizens of Mentone raised the money to buy a headstone for Granny Dollar's grave. Shortly after her headstone was placed, sightings of Granny Dollar decreased dramatically. Although Granny Dollar is seen less often, Buster is still a frequent sighting in the area around DeSoto Falls and around the remains of their cabin. People visiting the area are often startled by the barks and growls of a large, angry dog. They hear him crashing through the woods as he runs toward them, but he is never seen as he runs around them. Other times, Buster is seen walking along the roads or quietly slinking into the woods.

If you visit the Mentone area, particularly around DeSoto Falls, don't be surprised if you see an old woman out walking with her dog. Or maybe, you will see only a large black dog roaming the nearby woods. Don't be surprised if he disappears before your very eyes.

The vine-covered ruins of Granny Dollar's cabin can be seen today just off Dekalb County Highway 156. DeSoto Falls is open daily during daylight hours to visitors. A part of DeSoto State Park, it is about seven miles from the main state park, just outside Mentone, Alabama. From the Lookout Mountain Parkway, turn south on Highway 613. Continue to DeSoto Falls Road, which ends in the parking area.

Little River Canyon
Little River Canyon National Preserve
CHEROKEE COUNTY, ALABAMA

Beginning on Lookout Mountain near Chattanooga, Tennessee, and winding its way through Northern Georgia and into Alabama, the Little River is unique among rivers in that it runs the majority of its course on a mountaintop. One of the cleanest rivers in the United States, the Little River creates a landscape of creeks, sandstone bluffs, majestic waterfalls, and, finally, the Canyon. Little River Canyon is the largest and deepest canyon east of the Mississippi, spanning eighteen miles and reaching depths of up to 600 feet. The Canyon was established as a national preserve by the National Park System in 1992.

For all its breathtaking beauty, the Canyon remains a place of mystery. On quiet, foggy nights, visitors to the canyon report hearing a distant rumbling noise. Could it be the sound of distant cannons or the marching feet of soldiers? When General W. T. Sherman arrived in Gaylesville, Alabama, in October 1864, he reported having 60,000 men in the Little River/Gaylesville area. Sherman actually skirmished with Hood's men across the Little River. The Canyon received its original name, May's Gulf, from Union General Andrew May. May and his men were assaulted by Confederate troops when attempting to cross the canyon to meet up with Sherman. Perhaps the spirits of long ago soldiers remain in the canyon fighting a war long ended.

Long before the war, the Canyon was home to Native Indians. Favored hunting grounds of the Cherokee, the canyon was believed to be home to a secret Cherokee lead mine. The mine was never found, and legend circulated that those who searched for it never returned.

Little River Canyon,
largest canyon east of the
Mississippi, c. 2015.

Mushroom Rock, one of the most famous features of Little River Canyon. When workers were building Scenic Highway 176, they were so fascinated by the natural formation they ignored orders to blast it and built the highway around it instead, c. 2015. *Courtesy David Jefferson Davis Jr.*

Settlers declared that their dogs would not even enter the mouth of the mysterious canyon.

On cold winter days, a lone Native Indian man walks out of the fog to peer over the edge of the canyon. After a few moments, he silently walks into the forest and disappears. He has been seen many times here, but only in winter. He does not acknowledge onlookers. He never makes a sound.

The remains of a church can be found near the canyon. Thrill-seeking teens have visited the church on balmy southern nights seeking ghosts, only to flee in terror when loud voices began emanating from the ruins.

One of the most interesting stories of the canyon is the legend of Littlefoot. From the late 1960s until the early 1980s a small amusement park known as Canyonland Park operated in the canyon. Operating form Eberhardt Point, one of the features of the park was a small zoo. Depending on who tells the story, either the animals were being transported and a few escaped, or all the animals were deliberately turned out into the wild. The outcome is the same: small ape-like creatures have been spotted in the forests surrounding the canyon. A group of Boy Scouts was pelted playfully with pinecones as they hiked the canyon floor. Rafters reported being followed by shadowy creatures that moved along the treetops. One visitor took a blurry photo of a small, hairy creature pulling what appeared to be an igloo cooler along the canyon floor. A group of hikers left their backpacks behind while they explored the canyon. When they returned, their snacks were missing and the ground was covered in tiny footprints.

Do spirits from the past still roam in this wild and beautiful place? Do creatures unseen follow unsuspecting visitors? There are areas in the canyon so remote and inaccessible that their mysteries may never be revealed. Their answers may remain with those who entered . . . and never returned.

The chair lift at Canyonland sits as a lone reminder of a once-thriving amusement park. The chair lift took visitors over the canyon's rim and into the canyon below. The park was also home to a campground and zoo, c. 2015.

CHAPTER NINE

UNDISCLOSED LOCATION

The Nursing Home

Nursing homes carry an aura of sadness. Many people see them as the last stop on the road to eternity. When an elderly person can no longer be cared for by family, nursing homes may be the only option. It is a sad fact that these homes are the final residence of many people, and many die while in care there. It would stand to reason that some of these spirits often remain in the nursing home.

One such nursing home in Northwest Georgia is home to many spirits. Its location must remain anonymous. The head administrator does not believe in ghosts for religious reasons and any employee who discusses the ghosts on the premises puts his/her job in danger. However, denying their existence doesn't make them go away.

One of the most prominent ghosts in the home is that of a former nurse. Wearing a white starched uniform and cap from years past, she walks the halls to this day, still checking on the residents in her charge.

Donna Christopher remembers the first time she saw the mysterious nurse. "I was working 11-7 shift on A-hall, during the '90s. A little man turned his light on and I answered it. He asked me who the lady was that kept coming into his room and standing at the foot of his bed. He described her as tall in a white dress and wearing a cap. I told him not to worry, she was just making her rounds. He died in two weeks. It was after that I saw the same nurse standing in 111.

"Over the years when I have told this, nurses have laughed—until they see her. She sometimes is at the end of the hallway. Two nurses told me they always thought I was crazy until they saw her, too. The last time I saw her I caught a glimpse of her standing in the activity room. One nurse recently spotted her on F-hall and one saw her in the independent dining room."

Who is this mysterious nurse from bygone days who still walks the halls of the nursing home? Perhaps she loved her job so much that she remains to this day, still watching over the residents.

The nurse isn't the only spirit that haunts this nursing home. An angel has even been spotted walking the halls. According to Donna, a resident in the home asked about the well-being of another resident just down the hall in room 100. Her nurse, Sara, replied, "I just checked on her. She is fine."

The resident then replied, "Well you need to go check on her again; the Death Angel just went out my window."

At that same moment, another resident approached the nurse's desk and informed the nurse that she needed to go check on the lady in 100 because she had just seen an angel going down the hallway. When Sara went into room 100, the lady was dead. Had an angel really come to take the lady in room 100 home?

A well-known doctor in the community died many years ago in the hospital near the nursing home. Many witnesses have seen him still making his rounds, checking on the residents. He doesn't talk to anyone, just silently walks the hallways, still doing the job he once loved.

The spirit of a little girl has also been seen by visitors and residents alike. Several residents have asked about a little girl that even comes into their rooms and plays. Who could she be? Could she be a spirit visiting from one of the homes nearby? Or from a cemetery down the street? Some believe she may have passed away in the hospital that once stood nearby. No one knows who she is for certain, but, if you visit a nursing home in Northwest Georgia and see a little girl in old-fashioned clothing playing quietly, don't be quick to assume that she is a visitor. She might be a permanent resident....

BIBLIOGRAPHY

and Recommended Reading

Cliett, Linda. "Nancy Emmaline 'Granny Dollar' Callahan Dollar." Find a Grave. Accessed October 17, 2015. www.findagrave.com/cgi-bin/fg.cgi?page=gr&GRid=62413002.

Cox, Dale. "Desoto Falls—Mentone, Alabama: Waterfall on Lookout Mountain." Explore Southern History. Last Update June 20, 2014. www.exploresouthernhistory.com/desotofalls1.html.

Cox, Dale. "The Ghost of Allatoona Pass." Explore Southern History. 2001. Last updated October 15, 2014. www.exploresouthernhistory.com/allatoonaghost.html.

Desmond, Jerry R. *Georgia's Rome: A Brief History*. Charleston: The History Press, 2008.

Etowah Valley Historical Society. "The Unknown Hero of Allatoona Pass." 2015. http://evhsonline.org/bartow-history/civil-war/the-unknown-hero-of-allatoona-pass.

Georgia Division Reenactor's Association. "Resaca Confederate Cemetery." The Battle of Resaca Reenactment. 2015. www.georgiadivision.org/bor_resaca_cemetery.html.

Hannah, Mark. "The Town Crier: Incident at Varnell," *Dalton Daily Citizen*. 2011. www.daltondailycitizen.com/news/lifestyles/the-town-crier-incident-at-varnell/article_d1a9e376-abf0-5b0f-a711-007466520cc6.html.

Hillhouse, Larry. *Ghosts of Lookout Mountain*. Weaver, IA: Quixote Press, 2009.

Historical Marker Database. "Opera Alley." 2015. www.hmdb.org/Marker.asp?Marker=12318.

Patterson, L. E. *True Ghosts of Northwest Georgia*. Dunwoody: L. E. Patterson Jr., 1982.

Penot, Jessica and Amy Petulla, *Haunted Chattanooga*. Charleston: The History Press, 2011.

Ronner, John. "Ghostly Hands, Flashing Lights, Eerie Thumps on Wall," *Rome News Tribune*, October 31, 1973.

Ronnow, Karin. "Floyd Ghosts Return." *Rome News Tribune*, October 31, 1991.

Scarborough, Alex. "Stories of the Supernatural: Ghosts of the Historic DeSoto Theatre Come to Life." *Rome News Tribune*. October 30, 2009.

Scott, Robin L. *Rome, Georgia in Vintage Postcards.* (Postcard History Series.) Charleston: Arcadia Publishing, 2001.

Tabler, Dave. "The Legend of Granny Dollar, Part 1 of 2." Appalachian History: Stories, Quotes, and Anecdotes. 2012. www.appalachianhistory.net/2012/01/legend-of-granny-dollar-part-1-of-2.html.

Tabler, Dave. "The Legend of Granny Dollar, Part 2 of 2." Appalachian History: Stories, Quotes, and Anecdotes. 2012. www.appalachianhistory.net/2012/01/legend-of-granny-dollar-part-2-of-2.html